Cupcakes

igloo

igloo

Published by Igloo Books Ltd
Cottage Farm
Sywell
NN6 0BJ
www.igloo-books.com

2 4 6 8 10 9 7 5 3 1

ISBN: 978 0 85734 9 828

Project Managed by R&R Publications Marketing Pty Ltd

Food Photography: R&R Photostudio (www.rrphotostudio.com.au)
Recipe Development: R&R Test Kitchen

Printed in and manufactured in China

Contents

Persian Vanilla

Prep and cook time: 30 minutes   Makes: 12

3 eggs
½ cup butter, softened
1 cup caster (superfine) sugar
½ cup milk
1½ cups self-raising flour, sifted
1 tsp vanilla extract

Topping:
1 cup icing (confectioners') sugar
1 tsp lemon extract
1 tsp vanilla extract
½ cup butter, room temperature
Candy floss

Preheat the oven to 160°C (325F). Line a 12-hole cupcake tin with cupcake papers. In a medium-sized bowl, lightly beat the eggs, add butter and sugar, then mix until light and fluffy.

Add milk, flour and vanilla, and stir to combine. Place in a blender and beat for 2 minutes, until light and creamy.

Divide the mixture evenly between the cake papers. Bake for 18–20 minutes until risen and firm to touch. Allow to cool for a few minutes and then transfer to a wire rack.

Meanwhile, combine all topping ingredients except candy floss, mix with a wooden spoon until well combined, and beat with the spoon until light and fluffy.

Place mixture into a pastry bag with a star-shaped tip and pipe onto all cupcakes. Top with candy floss.

Vanilla Rose Cupcakes

Prep and cook time: 35 minutes   Makes: 12

3 eggs

½ cup butter, softened

1 cup caster (superfine) sugar

½ cup milk

1½ cups self-raising flour, sifted

1 tsp vanilla extract

Topping:

1 cup icing (confectioners') sugar

1 tsp rose water

½ cup butter, room temperature

6 drops vanilla extract

miniature dried roses, approximately 8 per cupcake (available from specialty cake decoration stores)

Preheat the oven to 160°C (325F). Line a 12-hole cupcake tin with cupcake papers. In a medium-sized bowl, lightly beat the eggs, add butter and sugar, then mix until light and fluffy.

Add milk, flour and vanilla, and stir to combine. Place in a blender and beat for 2 minutes, until light and creamy.

Divide the mixture evenly between the cake papers. Bake for 18–20 minutes until risen and firm to touch. Allow to cool for a few minutes and then transfer to a wire rack. Allow to cool fully before frosting.

Combine half of all the topping ingredients except the roses, mix with a wooden spoon, add remaining ingredients and beat with the spoon until light and fluffy. Place the mixture into a piping bag with a plain tip and pipe onto cupcakes. Decorate with the roses.

Lavender Buttercream Cupcakes

Prep and cook time: 35 minutes   Makes: 1

3 eggs
½ cup butter, softened
1 cup caster (superfine) sugar
½ cup milk
1½ cups self-raising flour, sifted
1 tsp vanilla extract

Topping:
1 cup icing (confectioners') sugar
1 tsp lavender extract
½ cup butter, room temperature
2 drops purple food dye
candied lavender (available from cake decoration stores)

Preheat the oven to 160°C (325F). Line a 12-hole cupcake tin with cupcake papers. In a medium-sized bowl, lightly beat the eggs, add butter and sugar, then mix until light and fluffy.

Add milk, flour and vanilla, and stir to combine. Place in a food processor and beat for 2 minutes, until light and creamy.

Divide the mixture evenly between the papers. Bake for 18–20 minutes until risen and firm to the touch. Allow to cool for a few minutes and then transfer to a wire rack. Allow to cool fully before frosting.

Combine the topping ingredients except the candied lavender, mix with a wooden spoon, and beat with a whisk until light and fluffy.

Apply the frosting with the back of a teaspoon or a small spatula. Place the candied lavender on top.

White Chocolate and Buttermilk Cupcakes

Prep and cook time: 30 minutes

Makes: 12

3 eggs
½ cup butter, softened
1 cup caster (superfine) sugar
½ cup buttermilk
1½ cups self-raising flour, sifted
1 tsp vanilla extract

Topping:
100g / 4oz white chocolate, coarsely grated
1 tbsp butter
⅓ cup whipping cream
candied frangipanis (available from cake decoration stores)

Preheat the oven to 160°C (325F). Line a 12-hole cupcake tin with cupcake papers. In a medium-sized bowl, lightly beat the eggs, add butter and sugar, then mix until light and fluffy.

Add the buttermilk, flour and vanilla, and stir to combine. Beat for 2 minutes, until light and creamy.

Divide the mixture evenly between the cake papers. Bake for 18–20 minutes until risen and firm to the touch. Allow to cool for a few minutes and then transfer to a wire rack. Allow to cool fully before frosting.

Combine the chocolate and butter in a medium-sized saucepan over a medium heat. As the mixture begins to melt, slowly add the cream, then reduce heat to low, stirring constantly, until mixture thickens.

Remove from the heat and cool. Spread evenly onto the cupcakes with a teaspoon and then top with the frangipani decorations.

Triple White Chocolate Cupcakes

Prep and cook time: 40 minutes   Makes: 12

3 eggs
½ cup butter, softened
1 cup caster (superfine) sugar
½ cup milk
1½ cups self-raising flour, sifted
1 tsp vanilla extract
100g / 4oz white chocolate, chopped

Topping:
200g / 8oz white chocolate buttons
30g / 1oz butter
⅓ cup whipping cream,
½ cup butter, room temperature
½ cup icing (confectioners') sugar

Preheat the oven to 160°C (325F). Line a 12-hole cupcake tin with cupcake papers. In a medium-sized bowl, lightly beat the eggs, add butter and sugar, then mix until light and fluffy.

Add the milk, flour and vanilla, and stir to combine. Place in a food processor and beat for 2 minutes, until light and creamy. Add white chocolate and stir through the mixture.

Divide the mixture evenly between the cake papers. Bake for 18–20 minutes until risen and firm to touch. Allow to cool for a few minutes and then transfer to a wire rack. Allow to cool fully before frosting.

Mix ⅔ of the white chocolate with 1 tablespoon of butter in a medium-sized saucepan over a medium heat. As the mixture begins to melt, add the cream slowly, then reduce the heat to low, stirring constantly, until the mixture thickens. Remove from the heat and cool.

Combine butter and icing sugar and mix with a wooden spoon. Beat with the spoon until light and fluffy. Add the melted chocolate, combine, then spoon onto the cupcakes. Top with the remaining white chocolate buttons.

Vanilla Sprinkles Cupcakes

Prep and cook time: 30 mins   Makes: 40

3 eggs
½ cup butter, softened
1 cup caster (superfine) sugar
½ cup milk
1½ cups self-raising flour, sifted
1 tsp vanilla extract
1 tsp cocoa powder

Topping:
½ cup icing (confectioners')
sugar
1 tbsp hot water
sprinkles

Preheat the oven to 160°C (325F). Line a 12-hole cupcake tin with cupcake papers. In a medium-sized bowl, lightly beat the eggs, add butter and sugar, then mix until light and fluffy.

Add the milk, flour and vanilla, and stir to combine. Place in a food processor and beat for 2 minutes, until light and creamy.

Divide the mixture in half, and add the vanilla to one half and cocoa powder to the other, and divide evenly between the cake papers. Bake for 18–20 minutes until risen and firm to touch. Allow to cool for a few minutes and then transfer to a wire rack. Allow to cool fully before frosting.

Combine the icing sugar and water in a small bowl, and mix with a wooden spoon. Spoon the icing onto the cupcakes. Tip out the sprinkles onto a work surface and gently press each cupcake into the sprinkles.

Butter Choc Cupcakes

Prep and cook time: 40 minutes   Makes: 12

3 eggs
½ cup butter, softened
1 cup caster (superfine) sugar
½ cup buttermilk
1½ cups self-raising flour, sifted
1 tsp cocoa powder
1 tsp vanilla extract
½ cup milk chocolate pieces, finely chopped
⅓ cup whipping cream

Topping:
1 cup icing (confectioners') sugar
½ cup butter, room temperature
1 tsp pink food dye
sugar flowers (available from cake decoration shops)

Preheat the oven to 160°C (325F). Line a 12-hole cupcake tin with cupcake papers. In a medium-sized bowl, lightly beat the eggs, add butter and sugar, then mix until light and fluffy.

Add the buttermilk, flour, cocoa powder and vanilla, and stir to combine. Place in a food processor and beat until light and creamy. Add the milk chocolate and stir through mixture.

Divide the mixture evenly between the cake papers. Bake for 18–20 minutes until risen and firm to touch. Allow them to cool for a few minutes and then transfer to a wire rack. Allow to cool fully before frosting.

Combine half the icing sugar and butter, mix with a wooden spoon, add the remaining icing sugar, butter and food dye and beat with the spoon until light and fluffy. Add the frosting to a piping bag and pipe onto cupcakes, then smooth over with spatula and top with flower decorations.

Chilli Chocolate Cupcakes

Prep and cook time: 30 minutes   Makes: 12

2 small fresh chillies or 1 tsp
dry red chilli flakes

3 eggs

½ cup butter, softened

1 cup caster (superfine) sugar

½ cup milk

1½ cups self-raising flour, sifted

1 tsp vanilla extract

100g / 4oz dark (plain)
chocolate pieces

1 tbsp cocoa powder

Topping:

100g / 4oz dark (plain)
chocolate, chopped

25g / 1oz butter

⅓ cup whipping cream

chillies for decoration

Preheat the oven to 160°C (325F). Line a 12-hole cupcake tin with cupcake papers. Slice the chillies and remove seeds. Place the chillies in a cup with ¼ cup of hot water to soak for 10 minutes. In a medium-sized bowl, lightly beat the eggs, add butter and sugar, then mix until light and fluffy.

Add the milk, flour and vanilla, and stir to combine. Add ½ cup dark chocolate, cocoa powder and half the chilli-infused water and combine. Place in a food processor and beat for 2 minutes, until light and creamy.

Divide the mixture evenly between the cake papers. Bake for 18–20 minutes until risen and firm to touch. Allow the cupcakes to cool for a few minutes and then transfer to a wire rack. Allow to cool fully before frosting.

Combine the chocolate and butter in a medium-sized saucepan over a medium heat. As the mixture begins to melt, reduce the heat to low, stirring constantly, until melted. Remove from the heat, add the cream, remaining chilli water and stir. Rest for 10 minutes: the mixture will be firm and velvety in consistency. Put it in a piping bag with a small plain tip and pipe onto cakes. Top with fresh small chillies.

Chocolate Chip Cupcakes

Prep and cook time: 30 minutes   Makes: 12

3 eggs

½ cup butter, softened

1 cup caster (superfine) sugar

½ cup milk

1½ cups self-raising flour, sifted

1 tsp vanilla extract

120g / 4½oz milk chocolate drops

1 tbsp cocoa powder

Topping:

½ cup milk chocolate, grated

1 cup butter, room temperature

⅓ cup whipping cream

1 cup icing (confectioners') sugar

1 tsp vanilla extract

½ cup milk chocolate drops

½ cup small chocolate drops

Preheat the oven to 160°C (325F). Line a 12-hole cupcake tin with cupcake papers. In a medium-sized bowl, lightly beat the eggs, add butter and sugar, then mix until light and fluffy.

Place in a food processor and beat for 2 minutes, until light and creamy. Add the milk, flour and vanilla, and stir to combine. Add ½ cup of the milk chocolate and cocoa powder, and stir through mixture.

Divide the mixture evenly between the cupcake papers. Bake for 18–20 minutes until risen and firm to touch. Allow to cool for a few minutes and then transfer to a wire rack. Allow to cool fully before frosting.

Put the chocolate and half the butter in a medium-sized saucepan over a medium heat. As the mixture begins to melt, reduce heat to low, stirring constantly, until it has melted. Remove from the heat, add the cream and stir. Rest for 10 minutes: the mixture will be firm and velvety in consistency.

Combine remaining butter, icing sugar and vanilla extract, stir until light and fluffy. Add the melted chocolate mixture, stir in the chocolate drops and spoon onto the cooled cupcakes. Sprinkle with small chocolate drops.

Chocolate Toffee Cupcakes

Prep and cook time: 30 minutes   makes: 12

3 eggs
½ cup butter, softened
1 cup caster (superfine) sugar
½ cup buttermilk
1½ cups self-raising flour, sifted
1 tsp vanilla extract

Topping:
½ cup chocolate drops
½ cup butter, room temperature
⅓ cup whipping cream
1 cup icing (confectioners') sugar
1 tsp vanilla extract
½ cup toffee pieces

Preheat the oven to 160°C (325F). Line a 12-hole cupcake tin with cupcake papers. In a medium-sized bowl, lightly beat the eggs, add butter and sugar, then mix until light and fluffy.

Add the buttermilk, flour and vanilla and stir to combine. Place in a food processor and beat for 2 minutes until light and creamy.

Divide the mixture evenly between the cupcake papers. Bake for 18–20 minutes until risen and firm to touch. Allow them to cool for a few minutes and then transfer to a wire rack. Allow to cool fully before frosting.

Combine the chocolate and half the butter in a medium-sized saucepan over a medium heat. As the mixture begins to melt, reduce the heat to low, stirring constantly, until melted. Remove from the heat, add the cream and stir. Rest for 10 minutes, the mixture will be firm and velvety in consistency.

Combine the remaining butter, icing sugar and vanilla extract and stir until light and fluffy. Add melted chocolate mixture and stir to combine. Apply frosting to each cupcake with a knife. Top each cupcake with a cluster of toffee pieces.

Rocky Road Cupcakes

Prep and cook time: 40 minutes   Makes: 12

3 eggs

½ cup butter, softened

1 cup caster (superfine) sugar

½ cup milk

1½ cups self-raising flour, sifted

1 tsp vanilla extract

1 tbsp cocoa powder

Topping:

½ cup milk chocolate drops

½ cup butter, room temperature

⅓ cup whipping cream

1 cup icing (confectioners') sugar

1 tsp vanilla extract

¼ cup candied cherries, chopped

⅓ cup almonds, chopped

⅓ cup marshmallows, chopped

Preheat the oven to 160°C (325F). Line a 12-hole cupcake tin with cupcake papers. In a medium-sized bowl, lightly beat the eggs, add butter and sugar, then mix until light and fluffy.

Add the milk, flour, vanilla and cocoa powder, and stir to combine. Place in a food processor and beat until light and creamy.

Divide the mixture evenly between the cupcake papers. Bake for 18–20 minutes until risen and firm to touch. Allow them to cool for a few minutes and then transfer to a wire rack. Allow to cool fully before frosting.

Put the chocolate and half the butter in a medium-sized saucepan over a medium heat. As the mixture begins to melt, reduce the heat to low, stirring constantly, until melted. Remove from the heat, add cream and stir. Rest for 10 minutes, the mixture will be firm and velvety in consistency.

Combine the remaining butter, icing sugar and vanilla extract, and stir until light and fluffy. Add the melted chocolate mixture and stir to combine. Ice the top of each cupcake and decorate with pieces of cherry, almonds and marshmallows.

Black Forest Cupcakes

Prep and cook time: 40 minutes   Makes: 12

3 eggs
½ cup butter, softened
1 cup caster (superfine) sugar
½ cup milk
1½ cups self-raising flour, sifted
1 tbsp kirsch liqueur
¼ cup cocoa powder

Topping:
100g / 4oz whipping cream
12 fresh cherries
¼ cup dark (plain) chocolate, shaved

Preheat the oven to 160°C (325F). Line a 12-hole cupcake tin with cupcake papers. In a medium-sized bowl, lightly beat the eggs, add butter and sugar, then mix until light and fluffy.

Add the milk, flour and cocoa powder, and stir to combine. Place in a food processor and beat for 2 minutes, until light and creamy, then fold through kirsch liqueur.

Divide the mixture evenly between the cake papers. Bake for 18–20 minutes until risen and firm to touch. Allow them to cool for a few minutes and then transfer to a wire rack. Allow to cool fully before frosting.

Beat cream until stiff peaks form, then top each cake with a spoonful of cream, a sprinkle of chocolate shavings and a fresh cherry.

Apple and Cinnamon Cupcakes

Prep and cook time: 30 minutes   Makes: 12

½ apple, peeled and chopped into small pieces
1 lemon, juiced
1 tbsp cinnamon
3 eggs
½ cup butter, softened
1 cup caster (superfine) sugar
½ cup milk
1½ cups self-raising flour, sifted

Topping:
1 cup icing (confectioners') sugar
½ cup butter, room temperature
1 tbsp cinnamon sugar

Preheat the oven to 160°C (325F). Line a 12-hole cupcake tin with cupcake papers. In a small bowl, coat the apple pieces with lemon juice and sprinkle with cinnamon. In a medium-sized bowl, lightly beat the eggs, add the butter and sugar, then mix until light and fluffy.

Add the milk and flour and beat for 2 minutes, until light and creamy. Add the spiced apple and stir through mixture.

Divide the mixture evenly between the cake papers. Bake for 18–20 minutes until risen and firm to touch. Allow them to cool for a few minutes and then transfer to a wire rack. Allow to cool fully before frosting.

Combine half the icing sugar and butter, mix with a wooden spoon, add the remaining icing sugar and butter and then beat until light and fluffy. Spoon the topping onto cupcakes and sprinkle cinnamon sugar on top.

Orange Poppy Cupcakes

Prep and cook time: 30 minutes   Makes: 12

3 eggs
½ cup butter, softened
1 cup caster (superfine) sugar
½ cup buttermilk
1½ cups self-raising flour, sifted
1 orange , zest
½ orange, juice
1 tsp poppy seeds

Topping:
1 cup icing (confectioners') sugar
½ cup butter, room temperature
½ orange, juice
½ tsp poppy seeds
1 orange, zest
candied orange pieces, cut into thin slivers

Preheat the oven to 160°C (325F). Line a 12-hole cupcake tin with cupcake papers. In a medium-sized bowl, lightly beat the eggs, add butter and sugar, then mix until light and fluffy.

Add the buttermilk and flour, and stir to combine. Place in a food processor and beat until light and creamy. Add the orange zest, orange juice and poppy seeds, and mix with a wooden spoon.

Divide the mixture evenly between the paper cases. Bake for 18–20 minutes until risen and firm to touch. Allow them to cool for a few minutes and then transfer to a wire rack. Allow to cool fully before frosting.

Combine the topping ingredients, and mix with a wooden spoon. Spoon the icing onto the cakes. Top with candied orange pieces.

Blueberry Cupcakes

Prep and cook time: 45 minutes   Makes: 12

3 eggs
½ cup butter, softened
1 cup caster (superfine) sugar
½ cup milk
1½ cups self-raising flour, sifted
1 tsp vanilla extract
200g / 8oz blueberries

Topping:
1 cup icing (confectioners')
sugar
2 tbsps of blueberries, mashed
100g / 4oz blueberries

Preheat the oven to 160°C (325F). Line a 12-hole cupcake tin with cupcake papers. Lightly beat the eggs, add butter and sugar, then mix until light and fluffy.

Add the milk, flour and vanilla and stir to combine. Place in a food processor and beat until light and creamy. Add the blueberries and stir through the mixture.

Divide the mixture evenly between the cake papers. Bake for 18–20 minutes until risen and firm to touch. Allow them to cool for a few minutes and then transfer to a wire rack. Allow to cool fully before frosting.

Mix the icing sugar and mashed berries in a medium-sized bowl with a wooden spoon. Use a spatula to apply frosting to each cupcake and top with a blueberry.

Banana Nut Cupcakes

Prep and cook time: 50 minutes   Makes: 12

3 eggs
½ cup butter, softened
1 cup caster (superfine) sugar
½ cup milk
1½ cups self-raising flour, sifted
1 tsp smooth peanut butter
1 banana, mashed

Topping:
½ cup caster (superfine) sugar,
for toffee
1 cup icing (confectioners')
sugar
½ cup butter, room
temperature
2 tbsps crunchy
unsalted peanut butter
1 tbsp golden syrup

Preheat the oven to 160°C (325F). Line a 12-hole cupcake tin with cupcake papers. In a medium-sized bowl, lightly beat the eggs, add butter and sugar, then mix until light and fluffy.

Add the milk, flour, peanut butter and banana, and stir to combine. Place in a food processor and beat until light and creamy. Add the banana and stir through.

Divide the mixture evenly between the cake papers. Bake for 18–20 minutes until risen and firm to touch. Allow them to cool for a few minutes and then transfer to a wire rack. Allow to cool fully before frosting.

Place ½ cup caster sugar evenly on a baking parchment-lined baking tray, and bake in oven on 200°C (400F) for approximately 25 minutes until toffee consistency forms. Cool until hardened.

Combine half the icing sugar, butter and peanut butter, and mix with a wooden spoon, then add the remaining icing sugar, butter and peanut butter and beat with the spoon until light and fluffy. Use the back of a spoon to frost cakes. Drizzle golden syrup onto the cakes and top with toffee pieces.

Peachy Pieces Cupcakes

Prep and cook time: 30 mins   Makes: 12

3 eggs
½ cup butter, softened
1 cup caster (superfine) sugar
½ cup milk
1 ½ cups self-raising flour, sifted
2 tbsps peach liqueur

Topping:
1 cup icing (confectioners')
sugar
½ cup butter, room
temperature
1 tsp peach extract
1 drop orange food dye
1 drop red food dye
peach-colored sugar flowers
(available from cake
decoration stores)

Preheat the oven to 160°C (325F). Line a 12-hole cupcake tin with cupcake papers. In a medium-sized bowl, lightly beat the eggs, add butter and sugar, then mix until light and fluffy.

Add the milk, flour and peach liqueur, stir to combine. Place in a food processor and beat until light and creamy.

Divide the mixture evenly between the cake papers. Bake for 18–20 minutes until risen and firm to touch. Allow them to cool for a few minutes and then transfer to a wire rack. Allow to cool fully before frosting.

Combine all topping ingredients except the sugar flowers in a small bowl. Mix with a wooden spoon, then beat until light and fluffy. Spoon the mixture into a piping bag and pipe dots onto all cupcakes. Top each dot of frosting with a flower.

Strawberry Surprise Cupcakes

Prep and cook time: 35 minutes   Makes: 12

3 eggs
½ cup butter, softened
1 cup caster (superfine) sugar
½ cup milk
1½ cups self-raising flour, sifted
2 tbsps strawberry liqueur

Topping:
1 cup icing (confectioners') sugar
½ cup butter, room temperature
red sugar flowers (available from cake decoration stores)

Preheat the oven to 160°C (325F). Line a 12-hole cupcake tin, with cupcake papers. In a medium-sized bowl, lightly beat the eggs, add butter and sugar, then mix until light and fluffy.

Add the milk, flour, strawberries and liqueur, and stir until light and creamy.

Divide the mixture evenly between the cake papers. Bake for 18–20 minutes until risen and firm to touch. Allow them to cool for a few minutes and then transfer to a wire rack. Allow to cool fully before frosting.

Combine icing sugar and butter in a small bowl, mix with a wooden spoon until well combined, then beat with a whisk until light and fluffy. Spoon the mixture into a piping bag with a medium-sized, star-shaped tip, and set aside.

Pipe frosting onto each cupcake and decorate with the red sugar flowers.

Sticky Date Cupcakes

Prep and cook time: 40 mins   Makes: 12

2 eggs
¾ cup butter, room temperature
¾ cup caster (superfine) sugar
1 cup self-raising flour, sifted
¾ cup water
400g / 14oz dates, chopped
2 tsps espresso
1 tsp baking soda
1 tsp vanilla extract
1 cup ground almonds
½ cup walnuts, finely chopped

Topping:
1 cup packed light brown sugar
⅓ cup butter
2 tbsp water
1 tsp vanilla extract
50g / 2oz dates

Preheat the oven to 160°C (325°F). Line a 12-hole cupcake tin with cupcake papers. In a medium-sized bowl, lightly beat the eggs, add butter and sugar, then mix until light and fluffy.

Add the water and flour, and stir to combine. Add the remaining ingredients. Mix with a wooden spoon for 2 minutes, until light and creamy.

Divide the mixture between the cake papers. Bake for 18–20 minutes until risen and firm to touch. Allow them to cool for a few minutes and then transfer to a wire rack. Allow to cool fully before frosting.

Combine sugar, butter, water and vanilla in a saucepan. Bring to a simmer over medium-low heat, stirring constantly. Without stirring again, simmer for 1 minute. Remove from the heat, allow it to cool and spoon onto the cupcakes. Top each cupcake with a date and more sugar mixture. Heat the top of each cupcake with a blowtorch, being careful not to scorch the paper or the dates.

Caramel Nougat Cupcakes

Prep and cook time: 30 mins   Makes: 12

3 eggs
½ cup butter, softened
1 cup caster (superfine) sugar
½ cup milk
1½ cups self-raising flour
1 tsp vanilla extract

Topping:
1 cup icing (confectioners')
sugar
½ cup butter, room
temperature
100g / 4oz nougat

Preheat the oven to 160°C (325F). Line a
12-hole cupcake tin with cupcake papers.
In a medium-sized bowl, lightly beat the
eggs, add butter and sugar, then mix until
light and fluffy.

Add milk, flour and vanilla, and stir to
combine.

Divide the mixture evenly between the cake
papers. Bake for 18–20 minutes until risen
and firm to touch. Allow them to cool for a
few minutes and then transfer to a wire rack.
Allow to cool fully before frosting.

Combine the icing sugar and butter in a small
bowl, mix, and add chopped nougat. Stir the
mixture and then spoon onto the cupcakes
in mounds.

Pistachio and Lime Cupcakes

Prep and cook time: 30 mins   Makes: 12

3 eggs
½ cup butter, softened
1 cup caster (superfine) sugar
½ cup yoghurt
2 cups self-raising flour, sifted
1 tsp vanilla extract
1 courgette (zucchini), grated
½ a lime, juice
1 lime, zest
½ cup pistachio nuts

Topping:
1 cup icing (confectioners')
sugar
½ cup butter, room
temperature
1 lime, zest
½ cup pistachio nuts

Preheat the oven to 160°C (325F). Line a 12-hole cupcake tin with cupcake papers. In a medium-sized bowl, lightly beat the eggs, add butter and sugar, then mix until light and fluffy.

Add the yoghurt, flour and vanilla and stir to combine. Place in a food processor and beat until light and creamy. Add the courgette, lime juice, zest and pistachio nuts and mix.

Divide the mixture evenly between the cake papers. Bake for 18–20 minutes until risen and firm to touch. Allow them to cool for a few minutes and then transfer to a wire rack. Allow to cool fully before frosting.

Put the icing sugar and butter, mix with a wooden spoon, then add the remaining icing sugar and butter and beat with the spoon until light and fluffy. Add the lime zest and half of the pistachios and mix through.

Apply the frosting to the cupcakes with the back of a spoon and sprinkle each cake with a few of the remaining nuts.